i Hung Myself on the Moon

poems

by

YONNAS GETAHUN

'I Hung Myself on the Moon' Copyright © 2015 by Yonnas Getahun.

All rights reserved. Published in the United States by Yonnas Getahun.

All rights reserved. The use of any part of this publication transmitted in any form or by any means, electronic, mechanical, photocopying, recording, or otherwise, or stored in a retrieval system, without the prior consent of the author is an infringement of the copyright law.

Book and Cover Design: Vladimir Verano, Third Place Press

Front cover photography : © Peeter Viisimaa via istockphoto.com

Published by 12toRain Productions

Author contact: Yonnastgetahun@gmail.com

ISBN: 978-0-9903077-0-9

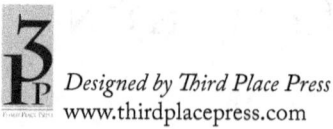

Designed by Third Place Press
www.thirdplacepress.com

To her

Especial thanks to Gavin Sullivan and Heather Dileepan for believing in me and this project.

Contents

Transgressions : 1

As Though I was Silent in Your Midst : 3

The Night is a Coarse Rose : 4

A Million Miles : 5

Not for a Dare or a Prize : 6

How to Serenade the Soul! : 7

The Full Moon and the Mounted Cannons : 8

$0.99 Triangle Heart : 9

In Praise : 10

We Learned to Howl Like Wolves : 11

Breaking Teeth : 12

Yellow Cherry Lipstick : 13

A Riddle : 14

Now that I am Infected : 15

Say Africa; Africa, Africa : 17

Contents

What of Your Wild Abandon? : 19

Hinged : 20

Quiet Now! Let Me Love You... : 22

The Way She Forgets : 23

The Distillation : 24

Across : 25

After a Period of Idle : 26

'Song of My Body' : 27

Wine and Lips : 28

I Celebrate You in My Body : 29

A Song Overheard at Laurelhurst park : 30

This is When I Write You a Letter : 32

Salvation and Tyrrany : 34

The River Begins : 35

Pop Poetry : Pop : 36

i Hung Myself on the Moon

Transgressions

I)

The raft cuts!
The lake wavers!
The fire burns!
The lightening yields!

Sex for a cabaret act.
I have returned
to my glory.

Arms reach!
Fingers crawl!

I command her
to kiss him.
She does.

My luxuries have become expensive
and I wonder
"how much should I charge for this?"

Laughter ensues
fills the chambers,
dries the wells.

II)

I have built
my own pyramids.
Which lovers to bury
along with me?

The sweet down under.

I have measured the distance
and my kite reaches the emblems
of the imagined,
past the house I believed
I was roofed under.

The moon, the Patriarchy, slanting
I have measured the distance
between lips and wolves,
deities of the night, and
evangelical promises
to wed my lovers in the desert.

Now THE PROCESSION AWAITS.

As Though I was Silent in Your Midst

A joke, a punch line
train ticket you cut
but a fare you never endure.
Magic carpet you board
but a kiss you never court.

I have made this.
I am set to destroy this;
unquenchable flailing and longing.

Like you wouldn't write a love poem
after you wed, after having children
after Pop's death.

I have become the ridicule
of my passions. I want
something better than this
than to be your favorite poet.

The Night is a Coarse Rose

The night is a coarse rose
and I whistle for the crime
we must commit.

Cherry-lipped cherubs
and bats look down on us.
Who still kisses when kneeling?

Stop taking notes please!
No one notices when
the doors fog blue.
My leather pants
and your scarf
to the wind.

Do you think
we can drown here?
"I'm not sure either".

Though, with grace and bow,
we shall dance in the privacy.
of this halo.

A Million Miles

I am a million miles beyond the sizzle.
Which way should I go from here?
Dust howls on barren fields.

A million years beyond the
pantomimes and plotters.
Where might your name appear on the marquee?
Vacant collars in line for the shoot.

A million miles from the roots.
Who should I trust with my delusions?
While dreaming, whom should I blow
a kiss to?

I am a million miles from the ruse.
A million years from the prized home comings.
A million winces from rights and wrongs.
Uncertain to return anymore.

Not for a Dare or a Prize

Must I abandon what I ask of you?
I could you show you but the night
and its hills tell it better.

Your rules are your inheritance
and you come with benedictions.
I reach for the door and my shadow
is burning. I am on the trail,
I promise.

Since words can fan the flame
I praise the mountain, and the sea
for their sadness. I praise Orion
who is aiming at the lazy eye
of the moon.

I can't tell any more
if the night is beginning or ending.
In the heart of winter
I can feel the back of the knees
of the spring to come.

How to Serenade the Soul!

The light invades my room,
I feel the hollowness
of my choices and sit erect.

There are mirrors where there shouldn't be,
like on your tongue. The way you speak
I can tap the rhythm of the river.

And call my madness beautiful.
Be quiet though, a poet is learning
how to serenade the soul.

The Full Moon and the Mounted Cannons

A trace of eye-lids, marking points
for your cycles, the full moon
and the cannons, the trail to embark
or emerge upon.

Clandestine exercises for the final procession,
all the same to the mute and the harmonious.
As if the candle asks why it burns,
as if the sky is really there,
as if there are bridges between ourselves.

$.99 Triangle Heart

The angles of your heart
the way it bends, for which
bruteness is a requisite.
Don't break what can be shattered!

The angles of your heart,
geometry elitism or defunct
perfectionism. The delusions;
yellow strawberries and witch
hunts for the moon.

And the prairies that turn
purple when you bleed,
become apostrophes for
entertained and fed.

The angles of your heart
stretching beyond conception,
become anchors of the end.

In Praise

I lie on the ground
and sense the curvature of
the world.

Your kindness requires no replication,
and I know I will disappoint you.

The body is a flag in the wind
wavering, one arm beholden,
one arm unfaithful & rebellious.

When I ask for explanation
you open a window.
When seeking perfection
you introduce me to the artisan.

When distraught you lay me down
weave tapestries of light and lightness.
When alone and abandoned
you rest gently on my chest.
I am dazzled so I behold
You spoil me enough
to remain unbroken before dawn.

We Learned to Howl like Wolves

Six years have passed since the war
the rocks still in place
we have learned
they keep us warm and safe

and yet the war implicates us
and they are killing
wolves in packs now
or breaking them into dogs.

Breaking Teeth

You are harder than the sea.
Father "go get her". Famished
trick, trappings of magic towers.

You never felt the beat when
the hunger set in. Scavenging
through the alley for ad-on
and ad-lib. The city and its
shadow was the key.

Ready to break your teeth.
"Check Mic, Mic check".
Now it is a party. Now it is fuck you.
Now it is pay me.

Yellow Cherry Lipstick

Let the musings and the stars
remain clamped to her brassiere.

Let the starlight and the flames
bury her refrain.

Let her soul's twin idly dance
between the razors.

I am a foreigner
mute to her pictographs.

I am a pair of dulled eyes in the
bantering sun.

Her folded knees and her
satisfaction
reign the evening. Let's praise
her becoming itches

and stay in the frailest of
paradise,

between reaction and
appearance of things.

A Riddle

My brother is hanging in there
but he is certain to die.
I lean on his favorite pillow
and pick at the guitar.

"Tomorrow is a riddle for a dying man",
he states. "Stumble in the dark
with a permanent swagger;

dance among the rubble;

burn little joint
remain solvent.

Remember the blue moon

is a brand of velvet and I
will paint you a line
a way to forget

the aspirations of the dew."

Now that I am Infected

Now that I am infected with
love,
not of its reputation, not by
its promises
but by its obligations and
open arms.

Now that I am a thief.
Now that I am shopping for
a knife,

and a husband.
Now that I am
looking for sex. Now that I
know what it is.
Now that I am on Freda's
end of Broadway.
Now that I am relenting, my
throbbing sanctity,
my city, my citizens, my
birds.

How all this must seem to you
my lovers of chained hands,
my beloved my exorcism,

my robin apple kicked to the curb,
my contemplative heart
and critical mind,
my addicted friend.

Say Africa; Africa, Africa

Of God.
Of mercy.

Of the calling
and called.
The veiled
and the blessed.

Of *you,*
the continuing perfection,
the servant.

The passing
of the pages
that burned
of the cities
that burned
of the lovers God sent.

Line of soldiers
trying to forget
etches of history.
Say Africa: Africa, Africa.

Say millions drowned
their feet shaking
our silence.
Africa, Africa...
Of malady.
Of malice.
Of melody,
of prayer.

A homeless moon
orbiting its haloed dissent.

What of Your Wild Abandon?

I can taste you on my finger.

    "What of the radius of the sun?"
I can scorch your wild abandon.
    "What of the gripes
    between wolves and the moon?"
I can taste the water and chocolate
    "And what of treachery and advance?
    What of the children
    and the forbidden retreat?"

I can dream of your victory.
    "What of our delight and ecstasy?"

Hinged

The poem that walks, that
tries to figure it out, that is
humbled and frowns on
interruption. The poem
that says be quiet and serenades

wells of sadness and longing.
The poem that confronts
the merry wind of love
and is humbled. That is American,
unemployed, undefeated

and still holding the violence
which is to say its presence.
Its position abstract and unruly.

The poem that contemplates
the heights as it looks
under the bridge, fancies
falling and surprising
the mystery and rising again
to dust itself.

The poem that befriends sailors, beggars
con-men and whores. That dances
frantically in the privacy

of its living rooms and attics
as though facing a deadline of regrets,
holding still even when certain
they will burn it out.

The poem contractually enslaved
with debt, it rose at Pearl Cafe
to explode with comics, troubadours and
howling wolves, where it sat alone waiting
for affection. Which burned to ashes walking
from Pioneer Square
to East Lake to the Ave
past the porno shops
looking for its name.

That is guilty for being here in the states
instead of the dirt fields of Kenya.

The poem...

Quiet now! Let Me Love You...

Quiet now!

I have found the dial tone,
the moon turns with in.
The thunder shakes
the almonds and apricots.

The sea is a parody
for the perilous and the wicked.
The sky wrestles the day
into night, all that purple

merging with the dirt,
its hands turn
to ecstasy.

In our rear view mirror
the road, the tar, and the wind

are swelling into a single atonement.
Let me love you...

The Way She Forgets

The way she forgets
her earrings, nylons
and Vaseline.

The train station is empty.
It is the crack of dawn
and my voice
is a fresh baked bread.

I sing to her
for all the times
I have been mute and for the
aching moments to come.

The Distillation

I don't want to look away.
    "Don't look away then"
I don't want to hold it in.
    "Don't!"

I am in love!
    "As memory or destiny?"
Rather as a well of tears, an uprising.

The door opens
Spring guides itself to her feet.

Across

It was only the other side of
the street but nobody goes
the distance anymore.
I can barely remember when
I last did.

Crayons on the coffee table,
the TV was full of static,
and Reagan had just won.
Something worth cheering.

My parents were asleep

when an insistent dream
dared me to go beyond the
door.
With a turn and a pull
I was initiated.
Hailing from the quandary
hoping to hitch a ride
anywhere.

The leaves were jostling the
wind and I was terrified but
alive.

After a Period of Idle

A thousand places to hide.
A thousand ways to pretend
to be still. A thousand
theories and arguments
to house myself in.

A thousand lies.
A thousand golden leaves
blowing-by.
A thousand mountains,
prairies, pyramids for
pariahs.
A thousand worlds I shall
never see and millions more I can't imagine.
Yet a single tremor,
the unplanned awakening,
a thousand kisses descend.

I rise to your lips and confess my final yearning :

"Teach me how to love or how to die."

'Song of My Body'

Where my right hip aches
and yawns, You point and
say "It is your origin."
I learn to listen.
My skin turning purple, a
hue of diamonds
with acres to plot and pluck.
I can smell the rose in the
moist evening.

I am planting my feet into
the ground.
The sky I attend to, the
emptiness a crown for
absence & presence.

Wine and Lips

Wine and lips,
the contours of which
the sky won't discern.

My hands are tied
to the ceiling
for touching you.

I received a memo.
The library is burning
and being chewed

by the wind.
The decent and the fearful
persist It is the Law.

Now my poems are seeds
for a new moon to rise.

Rise!

I Celebrate You in My Body

In the salted sun through the
lens when wilting in the
distance sinking with our
single heart

I celebrate you!
Past the rich men's lounges,
between the train tracks,
with Brooklyn beneath our feet

I celebrate you!
For all the unsettled ransom
notes I celebrate you!

With broken hands and a
fleeting soul I celebrate you!
You
 the song
I wake with on my lips.

A Song I Overheard at Laurelhurst Park

No love may deceive you.
No man may receive you.

My friend,
No brightness befoul you
No roads my cross you
No light can recite you
But love, love shall liven you.

No breathe may measure you
No land will claim you
No suffering can name you
No temptation may redeem you.
Ha?
But the wild shall guide you.
No civility can tame you
No beauty may fool you
No distance may reach you
No kindness will bless you
But the bridge shall alter
You. But the river shall sway,
drown and deliver you.

No peace becomes you
No victory can soothe you
No picture mirror you No
bond break you but the
hummm, hummm shall
clothe and protect you.

This is When I Write You a Letter

When my heart is on the
washing board
and my body is light as a flame
when my fingers turn gold
against the grain, or the
bedpost,
and the ocean begins anew
I write you a letter.

My inheritance; confounded
by what I am not rather than
what I am.

My heart is an orange traffic
light
too bright to deny.

I am shaking in voices now;
strings, and trombones, and
sketched lines and rousing
towers.

I am screaming into the void,
since your body has become
what I imagined.
That which won't turn the leaf,
sex can be so unfulfilling
when it is all the rage.

My feet are swollen but my hips
are ignited and this is when I write you a letter.

Salvation and Tyranny

Let's not seal this sadness
with lies. Let it linger as
scorpions in the desert for it
belongs here among the living.

Amiable, Cunning and Clever!
Let's not seal this sadness with
lilacs. Let it invade our costumes
as clouds cover the sky
for it belongs here amongst the ruins.

Amiable, Cunning and Clever!
Let's not seal this sadness with
promises. Let it be still among us
our guests our own failure and
mockery, salvation and tyranny.

Amiable, Cunning and Exquisite!

The River Begins

begins at a drought

with a plunge, a question why?

begins with a confession

"I love you" and your reply, "why?"

Begins with your mother

a stew of ashes and burnt bouquets,

with songs, and your fingers

in the flooded basement

The river begins with a contemptuous draft.

Pop Poetry : Pop

A lot of arrr, brew and beer,
multi topic barbiturates,
an ulcer going down the
throttle ahh, uhh, wee, no
body speaks French but
everyone has seen the sun set
there.

Hand full of popcorn and
oxycotins clothed well, and
inconceivable doing just fine,
a girl is talking suicide off

the
Tully's building. Another Pop
poet; pop zit;
her boyfriend, is cheering
"go ahead bitch see if I ...

Pop poetry; pop pop spit; Pop
poetry zit, Pop Pop pop
Poetry
you have made a fool of me,
pop

Two crows on the trail hop,
the carriage screeches
a camera gets in the way bibi
gun shot from the baby "he is
a natural" pop pop, poetry
feud, Pop! Pop! Pop!

(On that grassy knoll, the
shooter, it was a lack of
poetry, the interior substance
of being, that made him
shoot, pop pop pop.)

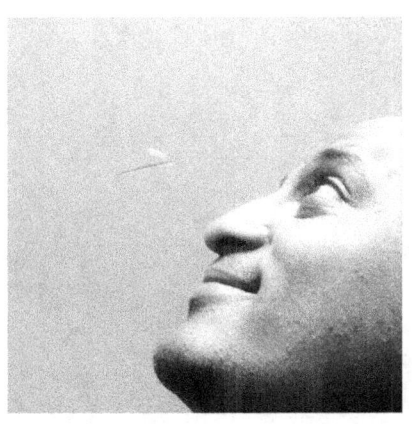

About the Author

Born in Ethiopia and raised in Spokane, WA, Yonnas has spent his life straddling worlds via languages and communities. He brings brilliant minds together for creative events and collaborations and has been writing poetry and performing slam and spoken word since 1999. He spent four years in poet collectives Urban Scribes Project & Basement Nation, and then self-published a chap book called "Serene Serpent" in 2004. Most recently, he curated "Touch Me I Am Violent" at Vermillion, "The Black Soundtrack" with Charles Mudede at NAAM, and NW Film Forum's "videOasis." Yonnas spends his time building bridges between Seattle's art and tech hubs, hosting and entertaining creatives and immersing himself in Seattle's rich literary, visual arts and dance culture. He is currently working on two manuscripts of poetry slated to be completed mid-2015.

www.ingramcontent.com/pod-product-compliance
Lightning Source LLC
Chambersburg PA
CBHW070441010526
44118CB00014B/2150